Your Body for Life

Mental Development

From birth to old age

Discarded

Anna Claybourne

Heinemann
LIBRARY
Chicago, Illinois

Edited by Andrew Farrow, Adam Miller, and Adrian Vigliano

Designed by Cynthia Della-Rovere

Original illustrations © Capstone Global Library Ltd.

Illustrated by HL Studios Ltd.

Picture research by Mica Brancic

Production by Victoria Fitzgerald

Originated by Capstone Global Library Ltd.

Printed and bound in China by Leo Paper Products Ltd.

16 15 14 13 12

10 9 8 7 6 5 4 3 2 1

Library of Congress Cataloging-in-Publication Data

Claybourne, Anna.

  Mental development : from birth to old age / Anna Claybourne.

    p. cm.—(Your body for life)

  Includes bibliographical references and index.

  ISBN 978-1-4329-7085-7 (hb)—ISBN 978-1-4329-7092-5 (pb)
1. Brain—Physiological aspects—Juvenile literature. 2. Mind and body—Juvenile literature. I. Title.

  QP376.C53 2013

  612.8'2—dc23   2012014550

Acknowledgments

The author and publishers are grateful to the following for permission to reproduce copyright material: Alamy pp. 4 (© i love images), 25 (Catchlight Visual Services/Hermien Lam), 26 (© Robert Destefano), 39 (© Corbis Super RF), 48 (© Mark Harmel FAP), 50 (© Tony Watson), 22 top (© Blend Images/JGI/Jamie Grill); Corbis pp. 6, 33 (© Robbie Jack), 41 (© Najlah Feanny), 43, 49 (© Imaginechina), 54 (© Grafton Marshall Smith), 45 top (© Serge Kozak); Getty Images pp. 27 (Dean Mouhtaropoulos), 28 (Photographer's Choice RF/ Reggie Casagrande), 31 (WireImage/Marc Grimwade), 32 (Jeff Gross); Photoshot p. 47 (MCT/Charlotte Observer/Todd Sumlin); Science Photo Library pp. 12 (Dr G Moscoso), 19 (CC Studio), 52 (Pasieka), 22 bottom (CCI Archives); Shutterstock pp. 5 (© CLIPAREA I Custom media), 7 (© Samuel Borges), 15 (© Kim Pin Tan), 16 (© Kurhan), 34 (© 1000 Words), 37 (© Vitalii Nesterchuk), 40 (© Symbiot), 45 (© Vician), 45 (© Africa Studio), 45 (© Sagasan), 45 (© Africa Studio), 45 (© Seregam), 45 (© Serg64), 45 (© oksana2010), 45 (© Dimedrol68), 45 (© Wacpan), 45 (© Wuttichok), 45 (© Anaken2012), 45 (© R. Classen); SuperStock pp. 53 (© Design Pics), 21 (© Blue Jean Images).

Cover photograph of brain anatomy reproduced with permission of Corbis (Science Photo Library/© Roger Harris).

We would like to thank Ann Fullick for her invaluable help in the preparation of this book.

Every effort has been made to contact copyright holders of any material reproduced in this book. Any omissions will be rectified in subsequent printings if notice is given to the publisher.

Disclaimer

All the Internet addresses (URLs) given in this book were valid at the time of going to press. However, due to the dynamic nature of the Internet, some addresses may have changed, or sites may have changed or ceased to exist since publication. While the author and publisher regret any inconvenience this may cause readers, no responsibility for any such changes can be accepted by either the author or the publisher.

Contents

Some words are printed in **bold**, like this. You can find out what they mean by looking in the glossary on page 60.

The Changing Mind

What does it mean to have a mind? It is a hugely important part of our lives. Your mind is the constant conversation you have with yourself in your head. It is the inner world of your thoughts, memories, and feelings—all the things you experience, wonder about, decide, and imagine. And, as you know, your mind can easily change. In fact, it changes all the time throughout your life—from before you are born to the day you die.

Teaching your mind
The mind consists largely of real-life experiences, things you have learned, memories, and feelings. Everything you do—such as learning and playing an instrument—can make your mind change and develop.

Growing and changing

Your brain is the part of your body that makes your mind work. Like other body parts, your brain grows as you grow up, getting more powerful and efficient until it reaches a peak when it works best and fastest. Eventually, it gets weaker and works less well. The changing brain affects the way your mind works.

Timeline: Stages of life
This book explores the many ways in which the mind changes and develops throughout life. These are the main stages it goes through.

Before birth:
It takes nine months for a baby, the baby's brain, and the first signs of a mind to develop inside the womb.

Babyhood:
From birth to one year old, a baby learns constantly as the mind starts to take shape.

Childhood:
Between one and five years, children learn to talk, walk, use their bodies, ask questions, figure things out, and come up with ideas. Older children develop many more abilities, such as reading and writing, and learn thousands of new facts, words, and skills.

Teenagers:
The ages between 13 and 19 are essential years for the brain and mind, as they go through major changes.

Early adulthood:
Even when you're grown up, you keep learning, and your mind keeps developing.

Middle age:
In their forties and fifties, many people's minds are working at maximum power.

Old age:
In old age, the brain and mind sometimes (but not always) stop working as well.

However, your mind also changes a lot throughout life for another reason: because so much of it is made up of real-life experiences, things you have learned, memories, and feelings. All the things that happen to you can make your mind change and develop.

The human mind

As humans, we are used to having a brain and a mind, but not all living things have them. Plants, fungi (very basic living things like molds), and even some animals have no brains and do not think. Animals without brains, and many animals with relatively small brains, mainly live by **instinct**, which means the things they do are programmed into their **genes**—the instructions that control the body's **cells**. The more intelligent a creature is and the more complex its brain is, the less it relies on instinct and the more it learns and changes throughout life. Humans have the most powerful brains of any living thing. So, the mind is more important for us than it is for any other animal.

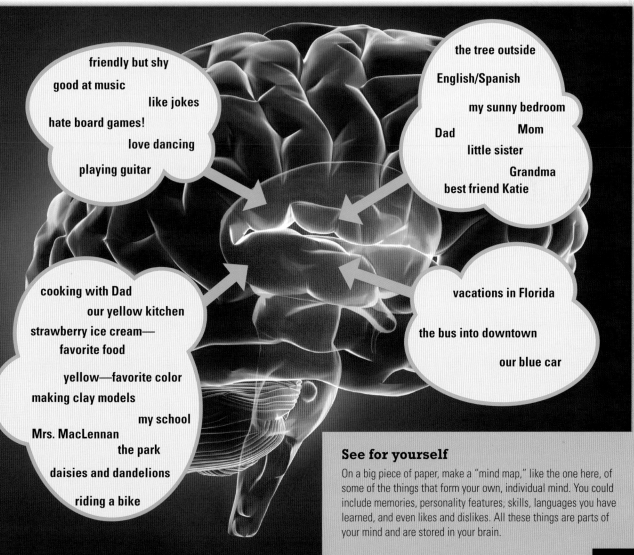

friendly but shy
good at music
like jokes
hate board games!
love dancing
playing guitar

the tree outside
English/Spanish
my sunny bedroom
Dad   Mom
little sister
Grandma
best friend Katie

cooking with Dad
our yellow kitchen
strawberry ice cream—
favorite food
yellow—favorite color
making clay models
my school
Mrs. MacLennan
the park
daisies and dandelions
riding a bike

vacations in Florida
the bus into downtown
our blue car

See for yourself

On a big piece of paper, make a "mind map," like the one here, of some of the things that form your own, individual mind. You could include memories, personality features, skills, languages you have learned, and even likes and dislikes. All these things are parts of your mind and are stored in your brain.

What is the mind?

Although we know what it is like to feel, think, and remember, scientists still argue about what the mind really is and how it works. We know that thinking happens when signals pass between cells in the brain (see page 9). But is the mind just a constant flow of these tiny signals? Or does it exist separately from the brain? Is there such a thing as the soul, the spirit, or the "self"? And how is it that we have **consciousness**—the ability to know that we are thinking? There are many different ideas and beliefs about the mind. This book explores what scientists have discovered about the mind, how the mind develops, and how it works.

It is very hard to say how the mind works—partly because the only way you can think about your mind is by using your mind! Scientists are constantly studying this and other problems. They may find answers that can help to explain more about how the mind does its job and develops over time.

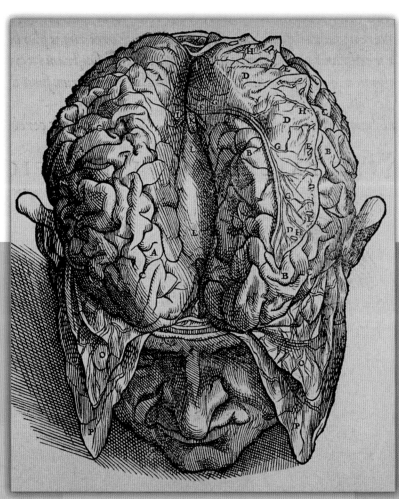

Where is the mind?

Long ago, many people thought the mind was based in the heart or even the intestines—not the brain. The ancient Greek thinker Aristotle, for example, thought the heart did the thinking and feeling, while the brain's job was simply to release spare heat out of the head.

But other ancient scientists, such as Alcmaeon and Herophilus, did believe that thinking happened in the brain, not the heart. By dissecting (cutting up) people's bodies and looking at the bits and pieces inside, they discovered that the brain controlled movements and senses. Sometimes they performed these dissections while the people being operated on were still alive!

What's in your head?

This picture of a head opened up to reveal the brain comes from a book by anatomist (body scientist) Andreas Vesalius, published in 1543. Vesalius studied the bodies of executed criminals, and paid artists to make detailed drawings of them.

Mental memories

The word **mental** means "relating to the mind," so "mental development" is the way the mind develops and changes. The words mental and mind actually come from the Old English word *gemynd*, meaning "to remember." If you think about it, memory is a huge part of what your mind is. You can only know and do so many things because you have learned about them and can use your mind to remember them. Without memory, you would not be able to talk, read, get dressed, or recognize your friends, your favorite foods, or even your front door.

Brain puzzle

What exactly happens between experiencing something in the real world and being aware of it in your mind? Scientists do not yet know. The way in which we become **conscious** of events around us is one of the biggest puzzles in science.

It can take from half a second to seven seconds for your brain to become aware of something you have experienced, depending on what it is and what else you are concentrating on at the time.

AMAZING BUT TRUE!

How soon is now?

You feel as though your mind is experiencing things in the present, right now—for example, when you are reading, touching, and seeing this book. But it takes a split second for your brain to take in what you experience, process it, and make you become aware of it. So, you never truly experience "now." Everything that you experience is already a little while in the past.

Inside the brain

The brain is the organ that thinks, remembers, and makes decisions—it is where your mind "is." In some ways, a brain is similar to a computer. The brain does these main jobs:

- It takes in information from outside your body, through your senses.
- It processes information, letting you understand things, have ideas, and make decisions.
- It controls body actions, such as making your legs walk or making your eyes focus.
- It stores all kinds of information, such as words, images, tunes, and numbers.

Even when you are not thinking about it, your brain is always active, controlling your body's basic life processes, such as breathing, growing, and your heartbeat.

The different sections of the brain are known as "lobes," and deal with different things.

Different parts of the cortex do different jobs.

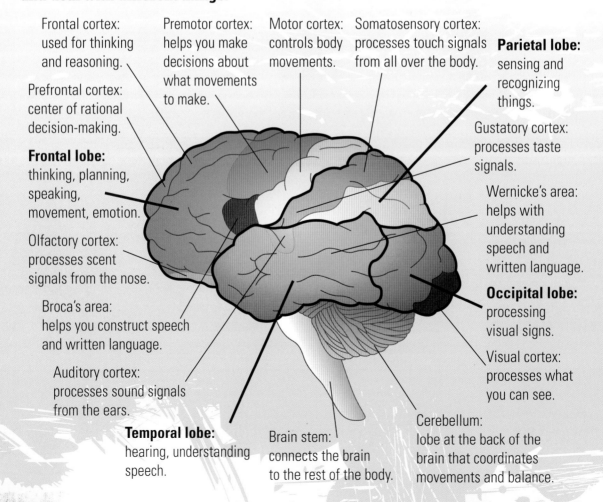

Frontal cortex: used for thinking and reasoning.

Prefrontal cortex: center of rational decision-making.

Frontal lobe: thinking, planning, speaking, movement, emotion.

Olfactory cortex: processes scent signals from the nose.

Broca's area: helps you construct speech and written language.

Auditory cortex: processes sound signals from the ears.

Temporal lobe: hearing, understanding speech.

Premotor cortex: helps you make decisions about what movements to make.

Motor cortex: controls body movements.

Brain stem: connects the brain to the rest of the body.

Somatosensory cortex: processes touch signals from all over the body.

Parietal lobe: sensing and recognizing things.

Gustatory cortex: processes taste signals.

Wernicke's area: helps with understanding speech and written language.

Occipital lobe: processing visual signs.

Visual cortex: processes what you can see.

Cerebellum: lobe at the back of the brain that coordinates movements and balance.

Half a brain

If you could cut your brain in half, you'd see these parts, which are found inside it. The cortex, or "gray matter," is the brain's wrinkled outer layer, and contains most of the neurons. The cerebrum is the main part of the cortex. White matter is beneath the cortex. It supports the neurons and carries signals between different areas of the cortex.

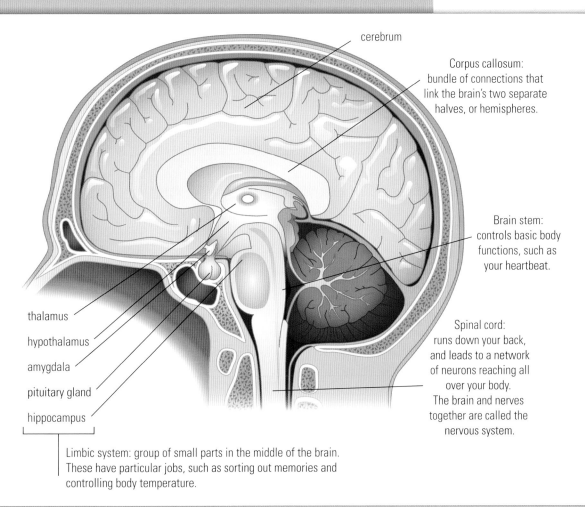

cerebrum

Corpus callosum: bundle of connections that link the brain's two separate halves, or hemispheres.

Brain stem: controls basic body functions, such as your heartbeat.

thalamus

hypothalamus

amygdala

pituitary gland

hippocampus

Spinal cord: runs down your back, and leads to a network of neurons reaching all over your body. The brain and nerves together are called the nervous system.

Limbic system: group of small parts in the middle of the brain. These have particular jobs, such as sorting out memories and controlling body temperature.

AMAZING BUT TRUE!

Brain figures

- A typical human brain contains about 100 billion (100,000,000,000) **neurons**.
- There are at least one quadrillion (1,000,000,000,000,000) connections between them!
- A normal brain can carry out trillions of calculations per second and is faster than the most powerful computer processors on Earth.
- Though the brain makes up only 2 to 3 percent of an adult's weight, it uses 20 percent of the body's energy supply.

Neurons

The brain is made up of nerve cells, or neurons. When you think, remember, or experience things, electrical signals are whizzing around your body and brain. They pass from one neuron to another in the form of special chemicals called neurotransmitters.

There are three main types of neuron:

- Sensory neurons pick up information through your senses and carry it to the brain.

- Interneurons process information inside your brain.

- Motor neurons carry signals from the brain to body parts such as muscles to make them work.

Neurons pass signals to each other along tiny branches, called axons and dendrites. A signal travels along a neuron as a flow of electricity. The neurons do not actually touch each other—they have tiny gaps between them. The place where a signal crosses the gap is called a **synapse** (see below).

How the brain changes

Neurons are very unusual body cells. Unlike other cells, like skin or blood cells, they do not keep dying and getting replaced. Sometimes new neurons can grow, but most of them form before you are born, and you keep them throughout your life. So, how can the brain and mind change and develop so much? The answer is that the connections between neurons change. New connections and pathways form, and old ones disappear. This happens all the time as you learn and experience new things.

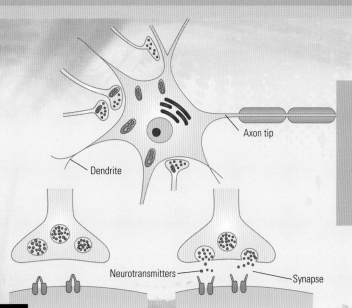

Axon tip

Dendrite

Neurotransmitters

Synapse

Neurons

This diagram shows how neurons pass on messages. The dendrites, or branches, of each neuron almost touch the axon tips, or ends, of other neurons. Wherever this happens, there is a synapse. At a synapse, signals pass across the gap in the form of neurotransmitter chemicals.

Learning

Learning is one of the most important things the mind does. It is essential for understanding the world around you, doing what you want to do, and becoming independent and able to care for yourself. It is the key to the development of the brain and the mind throughout life.

There are several different types of learning:

- Knowledge: This means storing facts in your memory.

- Comprehension: This means understanding things and being able to explain them.

- Skills or applied learning: This means learning to do a particular thing, such as playing a musical instrument.

- Affective or emotional learning: This is when experiences that make someone feel strongly have a lasting effect on the brain. For example, a child learns not to touch a hot pan because this is painful and upsetting.

Effective learning

When we learn, the brain transfers information from short-term memory into long-term memory. This works better if you alternate between different ways of learning and types of information, to activate different areas of the brain. It also helps to learn something, then practice it or teach it to someone else, which helps your brain to store it. We learn better if we are not stressed or distracted, so a good learning environment is calm and friendly.

Rest is also essential for learning. You cannot learn nonstop. The brain needs to process the new information while you relax, play, or sleep.

Making memories

What you learn has to be stored in your memory. There are three main types of memory:

- **Long-term memory**: This means things that are stored permanently, like people's names, language, or actions such as how to tie shoelaces.

- **Short-term memory**: This type of memory is more temporary. It includes things like what you had for breakfast this morning. You might know now, but you will likely have forgotten this detail by next week.

- Working memory: This type of memory lets you hold things in your head as you work. For example, while solving a math problem, you have to keep all the numbers in your mind and know which step you have just completed.

Babies

Everyone starts life as a single cell. By the time babies are born, nine months later, they have all their important body parts, including a fully formed brain. But how does the brain grow? And when does a baby in the womb develop a "mind" of his or her own?

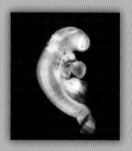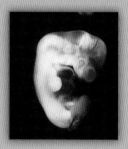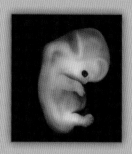

Embryo growth

The **embryos** in this picture are four weeks (left), five weeks (middle), and six weeks old (right). Even at this early stage, the head has formed, and the brain is starting to grow.

AMAZING BUT TRUE!

New neurons

To build the brain, the embryo has to grow millions and millions of neurons (brain cells). This mostly happens by the time it is five months old. At some stages, around 250,000 new neurons are being created every minute.

From a single cell to a brainy baby

0 days
A single cell starts dividing to form many cells.

4 days
Different types of cells start to form.

3 weeks
The neural tube forms.

7 weeks
The embryo develops an obvious head.

How the brain grows

When a new life starts to grow, the single cell splits into two, to make two new cells. Each of these splits into two, making four cells. Then they split in two, becoming eight cells—and so on. Very soon, an embryo with millions of cells has formed.

By a few days old, the embryo's cells have begun to differentiate, or become different types of cells. At about three weeks, part of the outer layer of cells rolls up to make a tube shape, called the neural tube, and one end of this tube gets bigger and thicker. This is where the brain will form.

Problems with development

Some health problems can begin in the womb if the brain does not develop as it should. For example, if the mother drinks a lot of alcohol (see page 34), the baby can develop fewer neurons, and some of the neurons that do develop may not work properly. This can cause learning problems after birth.

When does the mind begin?

An unborn baby cannot really "think" about things like we do, but some simple aspects of memory and learning do start to work before birth. Scientists have found that if they make a loud noise a few weeks before birth, a baby can hear the noise in the womb, and will wriggle and jump in response. But if they keep making the same noise, the brain gets used to it and stops responding as much. It can store the sound as a memory, learn that it is not important, and remember it.

Other studies have found that babies can remember the sound of a mother's voice, a song, or even a story that they heard weeks before they were born. After birth, the same sounds can help to calm them down—perhaps because they remind the babies of being safe and warm.

9 weeks
The brain has developed different parts.

10–20 weeks
Millions of neurons are forming to build the brain.

20 weeks
The brain has about a billion neurons, almost as many as an adult.

25–40 weeks
Mental development begins, with simple learning and remembering.

Baby brain

A newborn baby's brain is about one-quarter of the size of an adult's brain, and it weighs about as much as a grapefruit. It already has around 100 billion neurons, but the connections between them are still forming.

A new world

When babies are born, they are suddenly faced with vast amounts of new information. They are surrounded by lights, colors, noises, smells, a new home, and parents and other family members. Even things like the sensations of breathing, feeding, and wearing clothes are all new. A baby's brain is constantly taking all of this in, through senses such as seeing, hearing, and touch. Each new experience causes the brain to build more and more connections and pathways between its neurons.

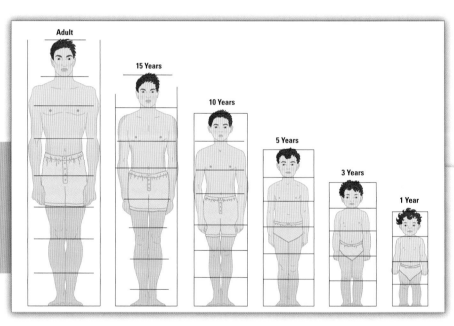

Brains and bodies
This chart shows how the size of the head and brain compared to the size of the body changes throughout life.

AMAZING BUT TRUE!

Bigheaded babies

Though a baby's head and brain are a quarter of adult size, a baby only weighs one-twentieth of adult weight overall. Babies' heads are very big in proportion to their bodies because humans have such large, complicated brains, and babies need all their brain cells from birth so that they can learn all they need to learn.

Our large brains and heads are one reason why being born is quite difficult for humans. Babies' heads have to be big enough for a large brain, but this means they can only just squeeze through the gap in the mother's pelvis bone. A baby's skull bones are not rigidly joined, so the head can be squeezed into a narrower shape to make birth easier. Later, the skull slowly fuses together.

Learning the basics

Babies do not learn things like walking and talking right away. First, they have to learn much more basic things, like how their body works and who is taking care of them. If you watch small babies, you will see that they wave their arms and legs, reach for objects, look around, and wriggle. This helps the brain to find out more about where body parts are, how to control them, and what different surfaces feel like. The brain then stores this information as more and more neuron connections.

Newborn babies also learn at a very young age what their parents or main caregivers look, feel, and smell like, and they prefer to be with them. This is known as bonding or imprinting, and it happens in many other animals as well as humans.

Things to do

We give babies toys to touch, mobiles to look at, and interesting textures to feel because they enjoy them. They are drawn to these experiences because they help the brain to grow and learn.

Love and the mind

Scientists have found that if babies do not bond closely with their caregivers, and therefore do not get lots of love and affection, it affects the way their brain forms. The parts of the brain that deal with emotions and coping with changes do not develop as well. This can make people more likely to suffer from mental illness when they grow up. The brains of children brought up without love and affection are also smaller than the brains of children from loving, stimulating homes.

The first year

Throughout the first year of a baby's life, the brain keeps making new connections at an amazing rate. In addition to taking in information, babies gradually learn to control their movements and interact with the world around them. In the first year of life, babies learn to do a lot of the activities that they will need throughout life— like smiling, getting around, holding objects, eating, and copying other people.

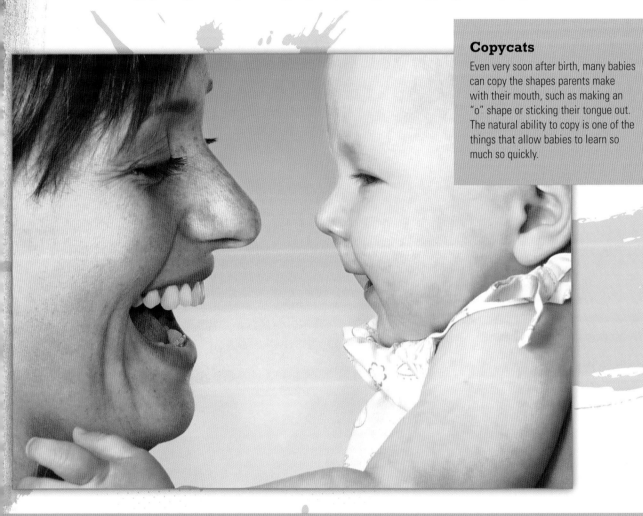

Copycats

Even very soon after birth, many babies can copy the shapes parents make with their mouth, such as making an "o" shape or sticking their tongue out. The natural ability to copy is one of the things that allow babies to learn so much so quickly.

One amazing year

On average, these are the ages when babies reach important milestones:

1–2 months
Smiling in response to other people

3–6 months
Babbling

4–5 months
Recognizing own name

4–6 months
Rolling over

Communicating

Long before learning to talk, babies can communicate. At first, they can only cry to tell their parents that something is wrong or that they need something. But soon, babies start to copy the sounds and facial expressions other people make.

For example, by about six months old, most babies are babbling, meaning they are making sounds that are a bit like talking, although without real words.

But how does seeing or hearing something lead to being able to do the same thing oneself? Scientists have found that pathways between neurons can be activated by watching someone else doing something—just as they are when a person does it for himself or herself. This may explain how observing an activity allows people to learn to do it at the same time.

Missing memories

The first year of life is an incredibly busy time for the brain. So, why do we not remember much about it? Scientists think that there are different kinds of memories. The things babies learn, like how to copy a sound, are stored as brain connections. But to recall the details of a past event, we use the hippocampus, part of the limbic system (see page 9), to connect different aspects of the event together. The hippocampus is not fully developed until a person is about three years old—which could explain why we cannot remember being a baby. But we do remember a lot of what we learned then, such as how to talk and hold objects.

Moving

By constantly experimenting with their hands, eyes, mouth, and other body parts, babies build up the brain's ability to control the body. When babies manage to do something useful, like grabbing a toy, they will repeat it, making the brain connections for that activity stronger and stronger. In the same way, they gradually get better and better at rolling over, crawling, sitting up, and chewing food.

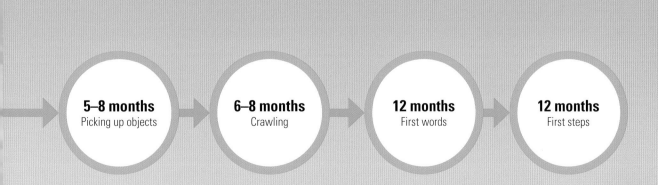

5–8 months
Picking up objects

6–8 months
Crawling

12 months
First words

12 months
First steps

Sleeping

On average, people spend about a third of their lives fast asleep. If you think about it, that is really quite strange! It means years of our lives are spent in another world—one that we still do not really understand. So, what are our brains doing all that time?

The sleeping mind

For a long time, most people, even scientists, thought sleep was just about having a refreshing rest. But in the 1950s and 1960s, scientists began measuring people's "brain waves" (electrical brain activity) while they slept. They found that several times per night, the brain cycles through different types of sleep. In one type, brain waves look similar to when a person is awake, and the eyes dart around under closed eyelids. It is called **REM sleep**, and it is when people have the most vivid dreams. Meanwhile, non-REM sleep, when brain activity is slower, is thought to help the brain store the memories people want to keep, by strengthening brain connections.

How much sleep?

Sleeping and dreaming help the mind develop by clearing out clutter and helping to store memories and facts. So, it makes sense that babies, who are learning the most, sleep the most—sometimes up to 20 hours out of every 24. The older people get, the less sleep they need.

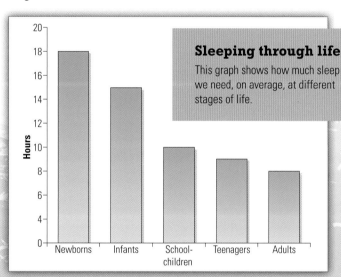

Sleeping through life
This graph shows how much sleep we need, on average, at different stages of life.

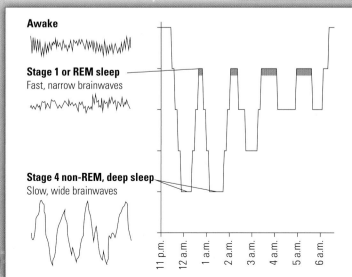

A good night's sleep
This chart shows the patterns of an adult's brain activity in a typical night.

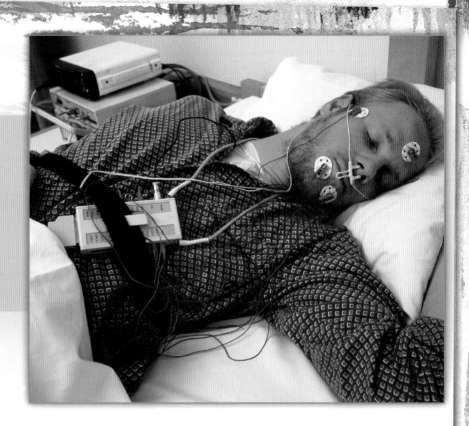

Dreaming

Dreams can be bizarre, yet they usually involve people, places, or events from real life. People may dream about flying or discovering a new room in their house. Most scientists now think that dreaming is very important. It lets the brain sort through everything that has happened to a person recently, as well as ideas, hopes, and fears, and to decide what to keep as memories. Dreams may also help people to get used to strong emotions and big changes, such as moving to a new home.

What do dreams mean?

Dreams can mean all sorts of things—or not much at all. But some common types of dreams do seem to be connected to real-life events:

- Flying: This sort of dream could mean you feel creative or are ready for a big change.
- Teeth falling out: This could mean you feel worried or unsure about a challenge.
- Drowning or being washed away: This might mean you feel overwhelmed by a situation.
- A new room: This could suggest that you want to try something new or do something differently.
- Falling: This could mean you feel out of control or not up to a task.

Children

Childhood is a time of huge changes in the brain and mind. Small babies learn a lot of basic, essential things, such as using their mind to control their body, recognizing people, and so on. But as babies get older, they learn new kinds of things. They take in more and more facts, such as the names of colors, letters, numbers, how to read, or the names of dinosaurs. They develop skills, such as telling time, drawing, climbing, or playing a sport. They also learn about who they are and how to behave.

Growing and pruning

From birth until about 11 or 12 years old, the brain makes more and more connections as children soak up huge amounts of new information. A three year old's brain is not yet as large as an adult's—it is about 75 percent of adult size—but it already has twice as many connections as an adult.

Meanwhile, a process called **synaptic pruning** begins. Neuron connections that are not being used often, or are damaged, stop working and actually disappear. This is not a bad thing—it makes the pathways of connections in the brain clearer, less tangled, and more efficient. Synaptic pruning happens throughout childhood, but the total number of connections still keeps growing.

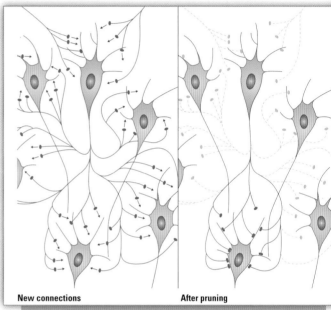

New connections   After pruning

Synaptic pruning

By age 11 or 12, neurons in the brain have formed thousands of new connections. A few years later, many have been pruned, while the ones that have been kept—such as those involved in speech and language—are reinforced and strengthened.

Childhood milestones

The mind can only manage certain tasks once it reaches a particular stage of development. Here are some of the milestones of early childhood:

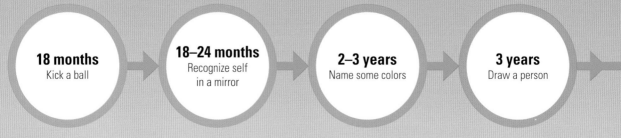

18 months
Kick a ball

18–24 months
Recognize self
in a mirror

2–3 years
Name some colors

3 years
Draw a person

Playing

Everyone knows that children love playing. Playing is fun, but it is also very important for the developing mind. It lets children practice all sorts of skills, such as following rules, using tools, moving the body, building, solving problems, sharing, and taking turns. All this builds more new brain connections. However, it is not just children who play—everyone does. Playing continues to help people learn things, develop skills, and work together, even as adults.

See for yourself

Try this simple test: Look at the two pictures quickly. Which row has more buttons in it?

A

B

You can probably see quickly that the answer is A. But most children will choose B until the age of about 5 or 6. Until then, the brain cannot easily distinguish between the amount of buttons and the area of space the buttons take up.

Building blocks
This tower game helps children practice building and balancing, planning, sharing and taking turns—and it's a lot of fun as well!

3 years	**3–4 years**	**4 years**	**5–6 years**
Tell simple lies	Feel sorry for other people	Hop on one foot	Tie shoelaces

Lots of learning

Children do not just learn things in school—they learn nonstop, no matter where they are. Their brains constantly seek out new information, so that they can keep making new connections. That is why children ask a lot of questions, love hands-on exhibits at museums, and find out everything they can about their favorite topics, such as horses or astronauts.

"Why?"

At the age of about three, most children go through a stage of asking "Why?" all the time. They continue to ask questions about the world around them throughout childhood. For the brain to develop properly, they need answers, which help them learn more and more.

Into everything
A lot of the "naughty" or dangerous things small children do are normal and natural—they are trying to find out how things work.

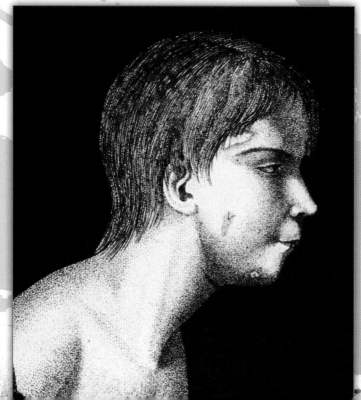

Raised in the woods
This is a drawing of a boy, known as Victor, who was discovered living in the woods near Toulouse, France, in the year 1800. He was about 12 years old, and had grown up alone in the wild. Victor went to live with a doctor who tried to teach him to talk, but he never managed to learn. What do you think caused language to be so difficult for him? (Read the next page for more on how language skills develop.)

Learning to speak

One of the most important things children learn is language. Between the ages of 1 and 10, a child learns 15,000 or more words, plus all the rules that make language work. Children's brains are very **plastic**, or able to change, so they can take in all this new information and store it permanently. But from the age of about 5, it becomes harder to learn to talk. And by the ages of 10 to 12, it is almost impossible. Children who have not learned to speak by this age can never master it. People can learn new languages after this age, but only if they have learned to speak their own language first.

AMAZING BUT TRUE!

Word magnet

Between the ages of about 5 and 10, a child can learn and remember up to 20 new words every day.

Intelligence

During childhood, it becomes clear that some people seem to think faster than others. Some are better at solving problems or understanding other people; some are very good at reading, math, drawing, or music. This kind of brain ability is called intelligence—but scientists do not yet agree on exactly what counts as intelligence, as it can affect so many different skills.

Many factors decide how intelligent a person is. These include genes, the instructions in the cells that people get from their parents. Genes tell the brain how to grow before birth. An unborn baby also needs a good supply of food and oxygen to grow enough healthy neurons. After birth, a healthy diet, being given loving care and attention, and having lots of different experiences as a child can all help to make a person more intelligent.

Child geniuses

Some children seem to have exceptional abilities in certain areas, such as math, music, or languages. The English scientist Thomas Young, for example, had learned to speak more than 12 languages by the time he was 14.

Learning difficulties

Some people have problems with particular types of learning and understanding. For example, children with **dyslexia** find reading and writing especially hard to learn. It is thought that conditions like this may happen because the brain gets wired, or connected, differently from normal at a young age.

Who am I?

As children grow over time, they develop their personalities. Personality is all the things that make people who they are—strengths and weaknesses, likes and dislikes, and behavior. It includes things such as whether people are shy or outgoing, messy or neat, creative, thoughtful, anxious, bossy, or forgetful—and thousands of other qualities.

But why are people so different? Personality is complicated. Some of it depends on the genes people get from their parents. Other parts depend on things that happen to people. For example, if people are raised to make their own decisions and help with chores, they will probably become more independent.

Self and others

When children realize they are separate from other people, this is a vital step in mental development. It begins at 18 to 24 months, when children first recognize themselves in the mirror. By about age five, most children realize that everyone has his or her own mind, thoughts, and feelings. This is called **theory of mind**.

If children do not develop theory of mind and learn to understand other people's feelings, it can cause problems. They can have trouble making friends, fitting in, and understanding how people expect them to behave.

The child is shown two dolls, Sally and Anne.

Sally hides a ball in her basket, then goes away.

While Sally is away, Anne moves the ball. She hides it in a box.

Sally comes back.

The child is asked: Where will Sally look for her ball?

See for yourself: The Sally-Anne test

The Sally-Anne test on the left can show how well a child has developed theory of mind. Try it yourself.

Young, preschool children usually say Sally will look in the box. They know that the ball is in the box, so they think Sally must think that, too.

Children over five years old usually say that Sally will look in her basket for the ball. Although they know it has moved, they understand that Sally has her own mind and does not know that.

Growing friendships
Making friends outside your own family is an important part of growing up. You can share interests and activities with them, and learn to support and care for each other.

Self-esteem

Self-esteem is how people feel about themselves. It is an important part of personality, because people's beliefs about their importance and what they can achieve will affect how they approach life. Low self-esteem is also linked to mental illnesses such as **depression** (see page 40).

Scientists have found that children develop better self-esteem if they are given affection and unconditional love (love regardless of their actions), so that they know that their parents love them no matter what they do, listen to them, and accept them for who they are. Skills such as being able to trust other people and achieve things without help are also useful in allowing self-esteem to grow.

Autism

People who have a condition called **autism** can have problems understanding other people's feelings and the rules of polite behavior. They often do not have theory of mind. Scientists are still unsure exactly why autism occurs, but it is thought to be partly genetic (caused by genes).

Autism affects about 1 in 100 people, and it affects more boys than girls. There is a wide spectrum (range) of autism, from severe to mild. Many people with mild autism can live normal lives. However, severe autism can make it very difficult for people to interact with others or make sense of the world.

Brain damage

The mind develops throughout life as the brain grows and builds connections. But what happens if something goes wrong? Injuries, illnesses, and other events can damage the brain—and that can have a big effect on how the mind develops.

Brain injuries: The brain is surrounded by a strong, protective case—the skull. But it can still be damaged in an accident. Head injuries happen most often in car and bike crashes and while playing sports. That's why everyone should wear a helmet when they are biking, horse riding, or skateboarding.

Some head injuries damage or even destroy a particular part of the brain. This can lead to problems like behavior changes, learning problems, or an inability to move certain parts of the body. Very serious brain damage can even lead to a vegetative state, when the thinking parts of the brain are destroyed. Although the person is still alive, his or her mind is no longer active.

Nail in the head

This X-ray photo shows a nail from a nail gun accidentally embedded in someone's brain—an injury similar to the one Phineas Gage suffered.

AMAZING BUT TRUE!

Personality reset

In 1848, a U.S. railway worker named Phineas Gage was injured at work when an iron bar, blown at high speed by an explosion, shot upward through his cheek and through his brain. Incredibly, Gage recovered and was able to live normally. But his personality changed completely. He had been a reliable, hardworking foreman. After the injury, he became so rude, impatient, and foul-mouthed that he could no longer find a job. This case shows how particular parts of the brain control particular aspects of the mind. Gage's frontal lobe (see page 8) had been damaged, affecting his personality and thought processes.

Concussions: Banging the head can also cause a concussion, a brain injury that happens when the whole brain shakes as it hits the inside of the skull. Scientists are not sure exactly how a concussion affects neurons, but it can cause memory loss and confusion.

Losing oxygen: The brain needs oxygen to keep working, because neurons, like all body cells, use it to make the energy they need. The oxygen supply to the brain can be cut off if a person cannot breathe—for example, if trapped underwater. After a few minutes, the neurons begin to die. This can cause permanent damage, such as learning difficulties.

Chemicals: The brain uses chemicals called **neurochemicals** to carry signals and control the way connections form. Some substances, such as lead, can upset the brain's chemical balance and stop it from developing properly. In the past, lead in paint, water pipes, and car exhaust damaged children's brains, causing lower intelligence, movement problems, and sometimes even death. Today, lead is not used as widely.

Brain repair

Some types of brain damage can gradually repair themselves, as the brain rebuilds connections. In some cases, the neurons can regrow as well. This is more likely to happen if someone is brain-damaged as a child, when the brain is still plastic, or moldable, and can change easily. After the teenage years, brain damage is more likely to be permanent.

Sports hazards

Professional boxers sometimes suffer from brain damage, caused by repeated blows to the head over many years.

Teenagers

The teenage years, also called **adolescence**, are well known as a time of change and upheaval. During this time, young people can feel especially confused and emotional, moody, angry, or passionate. They may be impulsive and take dangerous risks or become unusually clumsy, sleepy, or hungry. So, what is happening in a teenager's brain, and why?

Social teens

Teenagers are well-known for loving parties, late nights, and loud, wild behavior. Of course, not all teenagers are exactly the same—but on average, they do become more interested in going out and spending time with friends.

Back to basics

Teenagers might not like to hear it, but for the brain, the teenage years are somewhat like going back to being a baby or a toddler. The brain is still very plastic, or changeable, and a huge amount of growing and changing happens. It gradually transforms from being mainly a learning machine, which spends most of its time soaking up information, to being an adult brain—it does not learn as fast as it once did, but it is better at concentrating, creating, and making decisions.

Parts of the brain

As a teenager grows older, different parts of the brain are growing and changing in various ways. One of the most important changes is a huge amount of synaptic pruning (see page 20). Many of the connections formed in childhood disappear, while others become stronger and more permanent. Meanwhile, the corpus callosum, the bundle of nerves connecting the two sides of the brain (see page 9), grows stronger and thicker, making the brain better at comparing and analyzing various things.

Speeding up

The brain also goes through a process in which myelin, a coating on the outside of neurons, gets thicker. More myelin means signals can travel faster and the brain can think more efficiently. Scientists have found that this starts at the back of the brain and slowly moves toward the front. This could explain why teenagers can seem wild, excitable, or thoughtless. They are just as good as adults (or better) at things like seeing, talking, and making friends, as these are dealt with further back in the brain. But the prefrontal cortex (see page 8), which deals with **rational** decisions, is at the very front of the brain and develops last. In fact, the brain may not have all its myelin until a person reaches about the age of 25.

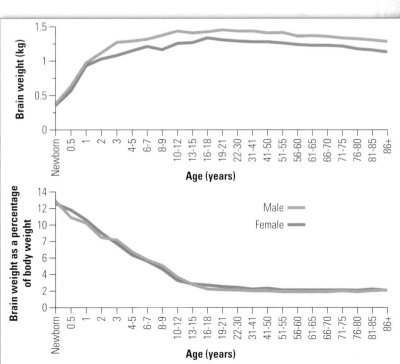

Shrinking brain
These graphs show how as you get older, your brain becomes smaller and smaller as a percentage of your body.

Use it or lose it

At the start of the teenage years, the interior of the brain is still very plastic, or moldable. But the process of synaptic pruning makes it more fixed and less able to change. Once the teenage years are over, people can still learn new things, but it becomes harder and they will not always "stick" as well. The things teenagers do often—like playing a musical instrument, playing soccer, listening to music, or computer programming—will form connections, skills, and memories that will probably stay with them forever.

On the other hand, if people stop doing something as teenagers, the brain connections for that activity will probably get pruned, and the skill or memory will be mostly lost. For example, if someone learns the violin from the ages of 7 to 11, but switches to the guitar at age 12 and plays in a band as a teenager, it will be the guitar skills he or she will keep for life.

Computer brains

Many teenagers play a lot of computer games. When scientists studied the brains of teenage gamers, alongside the brains of others who played much less, they found that the brains of game fans were different. They had a bigger ventral striatum, a part of the brain that deals with feeling rewarded and satisfied. However, it is not clear if playing games had changed their brains, or if teenagers who like computer games just have a bigger ventral striatum to begin with.

Hormones

Teenage behavior is sometimes blamed on **hormones**. Hormones are chemicals that the body releases to control the way it works, grows, and reacts to things. For example, the hormone adrenalin is released if a person is scared. It makes the heart beat faster so that a person can run away from danger if necessary. A part of the brain called the pituitary gland (see page 9) releases several hormones and controls other glands to release more. In turn, it is controlled by the hypothalamus (see page 8).

AMAZING BUT TRUE!

It's disappearing!

Overall, teenagers keep growing bigger and taller until about the age of 18. But their brains actually start to shrink in the early teenage years, as the various changes, including synaptic pruning, take place. Most brain growth happens before the age of 12.

In teenagers, lots of hormones are released to help the body grow and change from a child into an adult. They control things like the growth of body hair and the deepening of the voice. Some of these hormones can also affect the brain, moods, and behavior. Although they do not explain all teenage changes, they can make teenagers feel anxious, stressed, or easily upset.

Amygdala in charge

Brain scanning studies have shown that in a teenager's brain, the amygdala is more active than in an adult's brain. The amygdala (see page 9) is a brain part that is thought to regulate strong, instinctive emotions such as fear, anger, and desire. In teenagers, it seems to play a bigger part in decision-making, leading to what adults see as unwise, impulsive behavior.

Live thrills

At a concert, loud music and the thrill of seeing stars in real life can make some young people so excited, they scream hysterically or even faint. This is quite common, and big concerts usually have ambulances on hand.

Boys and girls

During adolescence, teenagers' bodies change a lot as they become adults. Physically, boys and girls develop very differently. But what about their minds? Of course, everyone is different—not all boys and girls are alike, and not all behave according to "typical" patterns. But scientists have found that, on average, there are some differences between the ways teenage boys' and girls' brains and minds develop.

Boys' brains

Boys have brains that are about 10 percent bigger overall than girls' brains. However, this does not make them more intelligent. They tend to have a bigger cerebellum (see page 8), the brain part that coordinates movements. They tend to use one side of their brain at a time for jobs like speech and spelling, rather than both together. And their amygdala, the brain part that deals with instinctive, emotional reactions, develops faster than in girls.

This may explain why teenage boys are generally better at physical things like throwing, spatial judgment such as figuring out locations and distances, and understanding systems such as engines. They are often less good at language skills, have a smaller vocabulary than girls, and take longer to develop discussion and memory skills. Boys are also far more likely than girls to take risks, act hastily, and behave violently, perhaps due to the amygdala.

Breaking the brain mold

Although the differences in how boys' and girls' brains develop lead to behavioral trends and averages, there are many exceptions to these patterns. There is nothing to stop girls from doing "risky" tricks on a skateboard, or boys from excelling in school!

Life imitates art

Teenagers often study Shakespeare's play *Romeo and Juliet* in school. It is about two teenagers who fall in love, but their families are enemies. Though it was written 400 years ago, the teenagers in it are immediately recognizable. The boys challenge each other, fight, and act hastily (as seen at right). Juliet is embroiled in emotional tangles with her family, but she makes careful plans for her escape.

Girls' brains

Girls' brains may be slightly smaller, but throughout most of childhood and adolescence, they develop slightly ahead of boys. They have a bigger proportion of gray matter, the neurons that do most of the brain's thinking and processing, and a more developed hippocampus, which helps the frontal cortex to work and helps to store memories (see page 9). The frontal cortex (see page 8) is the center of reasoning and making sense of things, and it becomes mature sooner in girls than in boys. The two sides of a girl's brain also tend to communicate more.

Teenagers and learning

Throughout most of adolescence, on average, girls perform better than boys at schoolwork. Their more advanced reasoning and language skills may fit better with the way learning usually happens in school—through reading, writing, analysis, and discussion. Some experts think that if teaching methods were more varied, or different things were taught to boys and girls at different times, it could help boys to do just as well.

As a result, girls are better on average at talking, reading, and writing, and they tend to know more words than boys. They are better at understanding emotions and dealing with several ideas or activities at once. Many brain-related conditions, such as autism, dyslexia, and **attention deficit/hyperactivity disorder** (ADHD), are much rarer in girls, perhaps because their brains tend to be more balanced and coordinated.

Tragic emotions

In *Romeo and Juliet*, the boys' strong emotions and hasty decisions lead to a deadly fight, with tragic consequences.

Case Study: Drugs and the mind

The word "drug" has many meanings. It can describe harmful, illegal substances, but also useful, often lifesaving medicines. Many everyday, legal substances, such as coffee, also contain drugs.

So, what is a drug? Basically, it is a substance that changes how the body works in some way—such as numbing pain, making a person sleepy, or making a person hallucinate (see things that are not really there). Whether they are swallowed, injected, or inhaled in smoke, most drugs enter the blood and circulate all over the body, soon reaching the brain, where they can have a powerful effect.

Alcohol overuse

Alcohol is one of the most commonly used of all drugs. It slows the brain down, making users feel relaxed, but also less alert and aware. Too much alcohol can make people behave dangerously and even fall **unconscious**.

Alcohol and the brain

The alcohol people drink is actually a chemical called ethanol. It occurs naturally when sugar in fruit or grain reacts with yeast and undergoes a process called fermentation. This is how alcoholic drinks like wine, beer, and vodka are made.

In the brain, alcohol interferes with the neurochemicals that carry signals between neurons, slowing down brain processes. It is called a depressant drug because it depresses, or reduces, brain activity. This can affect behavior in several ways, depending on how much alcohol a person drinks. Over many years, too much alcohol can also destroy neurons and permanently damage the brain.

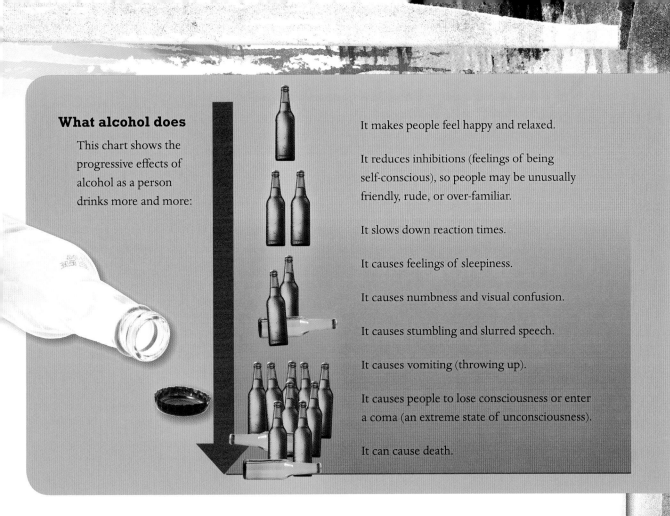

What alcohol does

This chart shows the progressive effects of alcohol as a person drinks more and more:

It makes people feel happy and relaxed.

It reduces inhibitions (feelings of being self-conscious), so people may be unusually friendly, rude, or over-familiar.

It slows down reaction times.

It causes feelings of sleepiness.

It causes numbness and visual confusion.

It causes stumbling and slurred speech.

It causes vomiting (throwing up).

It causes people to lose consciousness or enter a coma (an extreme state of unconsciousness).

It can cause death.

Drug addiction

Some drugs can cause addiction. This means that the brain gets used to the drug and begins to "need" it. Going without the drug can then make the user crave it desperately, or even become seriously ill, making it very hard to give up. Alcohol is addictive, and so are heroin, nicotine (found in tobacco), codeine (found in some painkillers), and many other substances.

Addiction does not always happen, and it can be more severe in some cases than in others. For example, while many people drink alcohol safely, consuming only small amounts, many others binge drink to dangerous levels or become seriously addicted. The drug diamorphine is used in hospitals as a painkiller, and used in this controlled way, it is fairly safe. But heroin, which is a form of the same drug, can be extremely addictive and dangerous.

Drugs and the teenage brain

Teenagers often want to take risks and rebel against rules, and many teens experiment with alcohol and other drugs. Unfortunately, the teenage brain is easily damaged by drugs, and teenagers have an especially high risk of addiction, because their brains are learning and changing so much. Taking drugs at this age can "program" the brain to become addicted more easily and interfere with the formation of important brain parts used for thinking and remembering. It can also make people more likely to become mentally ill when they are older (see pages 40 and 41).

Young Adults

As people grow up and leave adolescence behind, their brains go through a process of settling, consolidating, and practicing the skills they will need as adults. This takes quite a while, though. For many people, their twenties are still a time of change, adventure, ups and downs, and learning—learning who they are and how to deal with adult responsibilities.

What is an adult?

People officially become an adult somewhere between the ages of 18 and 21 (definitions vary around the world). However, the brain is still growing and changing in some ways during this period of life, and it only finally becomes mature when someone is about 24 or 25. From then on, the mind becomes more settled. The brain focuses less on learning and reshaping itself, and it gets better at thinking faster and more efficiently, analyzing things, planning, making decisions, and finishing creative projects. It is not a coincidence that this is also when most people tend to settle into the world of work, and many also become parents.

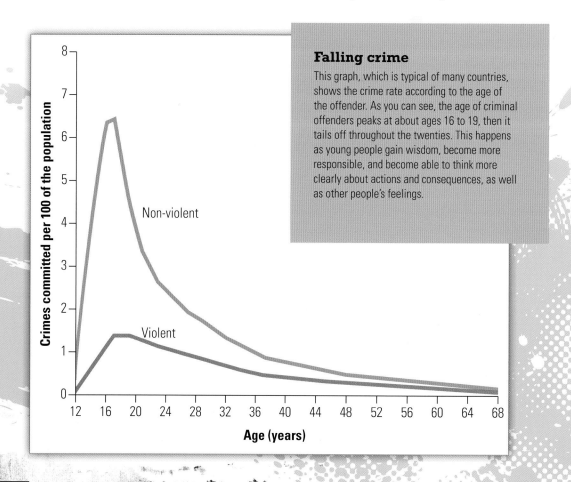

Falling crime

This graph, which is typical of many countries, shows the crime rate according to the age of the offender. As you can see, the age of criminal offenders peaks at about ages 16 to 19, then it tails off throughout the twenties. This happens as young people gain wisdom, become more responsible, and become able to think more clearly about actions and consequences, as well as other people's feelings.

Risk-taking

Very young adults, in their early and mid-twenties, are still much more likely to take risks than older people. This is partly because the prefrontal cortex (see page 8), which limits risky behavior, is still developing. It is also partly because it takes time to develop wisdom—making sensible decisions based on experience and practice. For example, young adults typically drive more dangerously than older ones, are more likely to take drugs, and are more likely to try adventurous or risky things such as bungee jumping or skydiving.

What do I really think?

As they become more settled and independent, young adults are generally less worried about fitting in and are less influenced by their parents. They often become more confident in who they are and may want to "find themselves"—that is, reflect on what they really think and discover their own individual preferences and personalities. They may want to experiment with new ideas—for example, they may reject the religion they were brought up with or develop strong political views that do not reflect those of their parents.

Brainwashing?

Brainwashing means using specially designed methods to change the way people think and feel, in particular to persuade them to join a religious group or political cause. It is a well-known term, but scientists are not sure if it is really possible to change the brain or mind in this way. However, there are religious cults and extremist groups that target young adults, at a time when they may be unsure about what they think and believe, and try to draw them in. This does not only work on young people, though. The people most vulnerable to being "brainwashed" can be any age, but they are likely to be intelligent, curious, eager to fit in, or in a stressful situation and in search of comfort.

Responsibility

As young adults get older, they often go through a lot of transitions, or changes, that require them to behave in more sensible, controlled ways. Getting a job, running a home, getting married, and having children all mean having to be responsible and "grown-up." These changes can be exciting, and they can help the mind to develop—but they can be hard to deal with, too.

AMAZING BUT TRUE!

I'm the impostor!

As people take on new responsibilities or get promoted at work, they often secretly feel that they are not really good enough—and that everyone around them has simply failed to notice. **Psychologists** sometimes call this the impostor syndrome. Studies have shown that it actually affects as many as 70 percent of people, who all feel as if they are the "impostor"!

Teenagers may feel their lives are stressful, but just think how many decisions, processes, and tasks a typical young adult's brain has to face every day. They might include any or all of the things shown in the image below.

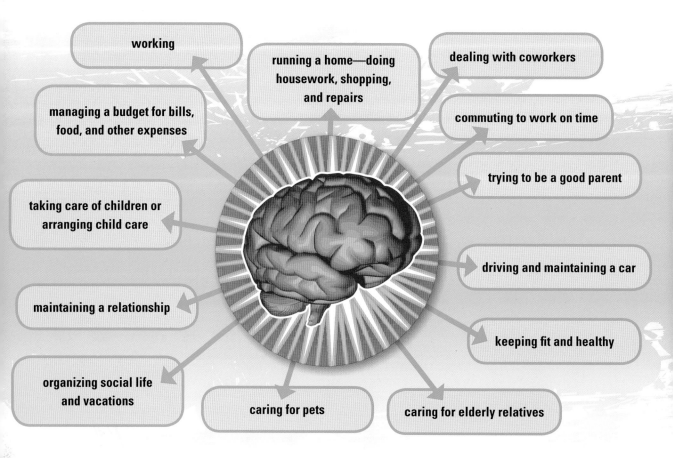

- working
- running a home—doing housework, shopping, and repairs
- dealing with coworkers
- managing a budget for bills, food, and other expenses
- commuting to work on time
- trying to be a good parent
- taking care of children or arranging child care
- driving and maintaining a car
- maintaining a relationship
- keeping fit and healthy
- organizing social life and vacations
- caring for pets
- caring for elderly relatives

This is a massive change from just a few years earlier, when young people lived at home or went to college, where someone else was often in charge.

Fluid thinking

Psychologists (scientists who study the mind) have identified two types of intelligence that are very important in adulthood: **fluid intelligence** and **crystallized intelligence** (see page 46). Fluid intelligence means thinking quickly and precisely, solving problems, using logic, and thinking about abstract questions such as "What is consciousness?" Fluid intelligence seems to peak in the twenties, and this is when many scientists and mathematicians do their most important work. Albert Einstein, for example, published his most important theories at the ages of 26 and 36.

Trouble in the mind

People who suffer from mental illnesses are often first affected by them in their twenties. Scientists think some people may be at risk of these illnesses from an early age. They are then triggered by life events and stressful situations in early adulthood. Illnesses that attack at this age include depression, **bipolar disorder**, and **schizophrenia** (see pages 40 and 41). It is also quite common for women to suffer from post-partum depression, meaning depression after childbirth.

Increasing stress

As people take on more responsible jobs, they often find that work demands more and more of their time, and causes them a lot of stress.

What is stress?

Stress means feeling pressured, overwhelmed, or anxious. Stress can be useful—it can make people study for exams or run away from danger. But too much stress, caused by things like a heavy workload or relationship problems, can make people sick. It can cause burnout, when people become so mentally and emotionally exhausted that they cannot function. It also contributes to mental illnesses. It can even affect the body by damaging the immune system (the body system that fights germs and illnesses), making people more likely to catch diseases.

Case Study: Mental illness

Mental illnesses are illnesses that affect the mind. They can cause unusual, troubling thoughts or feelings and make people behave strangely. Mental illness can affect anyone—in fact, it is very common. But because it affects behavior, it often carries a stigma, meaning a sense of disapproval by society. People may disapprove of, laugh at, or fear the mentally ill and use words like "crazy" as an insult.

AMAZING BUT TRUE!

Did you know?

At least a quarter of people experience some kind of mental illness during their lives.

Depression

Depression is one of the most common mental illnesses. It can make people feel miserable, slowed-down, worthless, or sometimes just blank and numb. It can lead to addiction, when people use alcohol or other drugs to distract themselves from their feelings.

Bipolar disorder

Some people have bipolar disorder, also called manic depression, in which periods of depression alternate with periods of mania, which means feeling energetic and excited, talking very fast, or making grand plans.

Fears and obsessions

Mental illnesses can sometimes develop when normal worries, habits, or fears become more and more important in a person's mind and end up taking over.

- **Phobias** are very strong, **irrational** fears, such as being terrified of open spaces, birds, or elevators.
- **Obsessive-compulsive disorder (OCD)** can make people obsessed with things like cleanliness, lining objects up neatly, or repeating special routines and rituals such as hand washing or chanting.
- Eating disorders such as **anorexia nervosa** affect people's image of their bodies and their desire to eat. People may stop eating altogether in an effort to control their body.

Worst nightmare

For an arachnophobia (spider phobia) sufferer, this tarantula could be so terrifying, they'd be unable to look at it—even though it's just a photo in a book.

Schizophrenia

Schizophrenia is a serious mental illness that affects perception and beliefs. Sufferers may see things that are not really there or hear voices inside their heads giving them instructions. They may develop paranoia (a feeling that people are scheming against them) and believe things that are not true—for example, that spies are following them or that their TV set is sending them secret messages. Schizophrenia can make it impossible to live normally.

What causes mental illness?

Scientists think most mental illness is caused by a combination of factors. Genes can place people more at risk—depression and schizophrenia both tend to run in families. Damaging childhood experiences, drug use, or a brain injury can affect the way the brain develops, making mental illness more likely. Life events such as losing a job, ending a relationship, or feeling constant stress can sometimes make people "snap," triggering mental illness in those who are already at risk.

Overcoming schizophrenia

John Nash is a famous mathematician who suffered from schizophrenia from around the age of 30. After battling the disease, he was able to continue with his career.

Rational and irrational

Rational thought is logical, sensible thinking, based on evidence and reasoning. Irrational thought is the opposite—it is thinking or believing things that do not make sense. In many mental illnesses, irrational feelings take over, even though the person can still think rationally, too. For example, people with anorexia, who are not eating enough, can see that they are very thin and that scales tell them they weigh too little. But they still believe they are too fat and feel afraid to eat.

Mental health

Good mental health is important for everyone. It is as essential as physical health for letting people do everyday things, cope with problems and challenges, manage work or studies, and have happy relationships. So, can mental illness be treated, cured, or avoided in the first place?

A lot of mental illnesses, such as depression, OCD, and schizophrenia, can be treated with drugs. These medicines do not work for everyone, but they can make a big difference. One example is the **SSRI** (short for "selective **serotonin** re-uptake inhibitors") group of drugs. In anxiety and depression, the brain may have lower levels of serotonin, a neurochemical involved in contentment and enjoyment. SSRI drugs work by helping neurons to pass on as much serotonin as possible.

Sometimes a mental illness like depression will eventually get better by itself. Drugs can speed this up or just help the sufferer to cope in the meantime. For some illnesses, especially schizophrenia and bipolar disorder, drugs do not necessarily cure the disease, but they can control it, making life easier and more normal for the patient.

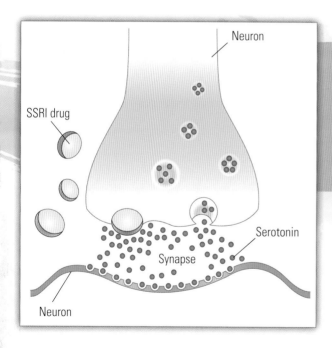

How SSRIs work

This diagram shows how an SSRI drug encourages the transmission of serotonin. An SSRI drug blocks the receptors on this neuron, so that the serotonin cannot get back in. As a result, more of the serotonin that is released gets passed on.

Talking and thinking

People with mental illnesses can also talk to a trained counselor or psychotherapist (an expert in mental and emotional disorders) and sort through their feelings. Being listened to and understood can relieve stress and encourage people to keep trying to recover. One type of treatment, cognitive behavior therapy (CBT), teaches the patient mental exercises to try to re-train the brain. For example, people with OCD can learn to spot when they are starting to worry, and they can distract their brain with mental exercises such as focusing on what they are sensing at that moment.

The dark side of genius

Although mental illnesses can be devastating, some are also linked to creativity and genius. Great artists and poets are more likely than average to suffer from bipolar disorder, for example. Famous artists, composers, and poets who are thought to have suffered from mental illness include Vincent van Gogh, Ludwig van Beethoven, John Keats, Pablo Picasso, Virginia Woolf, and Sylvia Plath.

AMAZING BUT TRUE!

Healthy body, healthy mind

Physical exercise, whether it is walking, running, swimming, dancing, or anything else, is very good for the brain and for mental health. In fact, scientists have found that exercise is one of the most effective treatments for depression and can often work as well as drugs. The brain makes chemicals known as **endorphins** when people exercise, which give the feelings of happiness and well-being that can help with recovery.

Staying healthy

There are quite a few ways to help the brain and mind stay well and reduce the risk of mental illness. These include:

- getting regular physical exercise
- eating healthily
- getting enough sleep
- avoiding illegal drugs and excessive alcohol and caffeine
- avoiding too much stress (see page 39)
- learning what helps with relaxation, and making time for it—for example, sports or music
- talking problems over with friends, family, or a partner

Intense impressions

The great Post-Impressionist artist Vincent van Gogh suffered from various mental health problems, which some people think contributed to his intense vision of the world around him.

Middle Age

The definition of middle age is not fixed, but people are usually seen as middle-aged from sometime in their forties to around the age of 60. The term "middle-aged" can sometimes be an insult, meaning uncool or out of touch. But like other stages of life, this can be a time of big changes, and the brain may be working better than ever.

Midlife crisis

People are often said to have a "midlife crisis" in their forties—but does it really exist? Psychologists think it does, although they may call it a "midlife transition" instead. During middle age, a lot of things can happen that make people feel alarmed and anxious, including:

- looking and feeling older

- children growing up and leaving home

- parents becoming ill and dying

- suffering a serious illness, or seeing a loved one suffer from one

- realizing that at least half of life is over, and believing they may not have achieved what they wanted to

In some cases, these things can cause mental illness or lead people to make big, sudden changes in their lives. For example, someone might leave a marriage for a new partner or quit a job.

AMAZING BUT TRUE!

Living longer

Not much more than 100 years ago, the average lifespan in North America and Europe was only about 48 years—what is counted today as "middle age." Now, life expectancy is almost 80 years. People live much longer these days because of improved nutrition (food choices), living conditions, and medicines.

Where did I put my phone?!

In middle age, people often feel their minds becoming a little less efficient in some ways. People may find that it gets harder to remember where they put things or to learn how to use a new gadget quickly and easily. This is because some types of brain function, especially fluid intelligence (see page 39), have already passed their peak and begun to decline. However, in some other ways, the brain is at its most powerful in middle age, as we will see on the following pages.

Seeking youth

Youth and youthful beauty are all around us in advertisements, TV shows, and magazines. Wrinkles and gray hair are often seen as undesirable. This is partly cultural, reflecting the values of a particular society. But it also has a basis in science: a youthful appearance is attractive because it signals health and fertility (the ability to have babies).

This means that becoming middle-aged can lower self-esteem and make people feel ignored or less useful. They may try to regain younger looks or behavior by changing their clothes, looking for a younger partner, or even having cosmetic surgery.

Signs of aging

Finding wrinkles, gray hairs, or thinning hair can make middle-aged people feel alarmed.

See for yourself

Try this simple short-term memory test on yourself and on family members or friends of different ages. Do middle-aged people score worse, better, or the same?

Ask someone to put about 12 different household objects on a table, covered with a cloth. Let everyone see the objects for a minute, then cover the objects again. Ask everyone to write down all the objects they can remember.

What are your findings? You may find that older children, teenagers and young adults perform better than older adults.

The mind in its prime

You might think of people in their forties and fifties as a bit past their prime, but in some ways, they have the most powerful brains of all. Younger people may think faster. But a combination of experience, knowledge, and learned skills make middle-aged people better at practical problems, controlling money, managing and teaching others, and creating great works of art.

Crystallized thinking

Crystallized intelligence is a type of intelligence identified by psychologists. While fluid intelligence (see page 39) is related to reasoning, abstract ideas, and thinking fast, crystallized intelligence is the result of past learning, wisdom, and practice at solving problems. This type of intelligence increases throughout life. Scientists think some types of brain power peak in middle age, when people have plenty of crystallized intelligence, but are not yet suffering from serious memory problems. Middle-aged people generally know more words and facts than younger people, and they are better at finding practical solutions to problems because of the knowledge they have learned.

This helps to explain why leaders of large companies, principals, senior politicians, and highly successful artists and authors tend to be middle-aged—because jobs like these tend to require experience, knowledge, and wisdom, rather than just analyzing and thinking fast.

New challenges

A midlife crisis or transition can sometimes have positive results, when people decide to make positive changes, train for a new career, or take up new hobbies or careers. For example, several people have left their careers as movie or TV stars in middle age to take up politics. Ronald Reagan, who became governor of California at age 54 and later became U.S. president, is one example. As this shows, the brain still has an amazing capacity to change and learn new things in middle age.

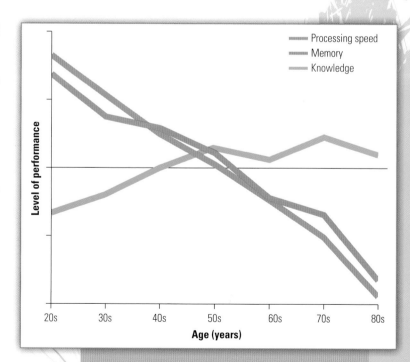

Up and down

This graph shows how some types of mental ability tend to fall through adulthood, while others rise.

Creative peaks

Middle age is when many writers, artists, inventors, and thinkers do their best work. This kind of creative work benefits from knowing more words, being exposed to more ideas, and having years of practice at concentrating, creating, and seeing projects through. Here are a few examples:

- English writer William Shakespeare wrote his greatest, most complex plays from the ages of about 36 to 47.
- Spanish artist Pablo Picasso painted his masterpiece, *Guernica*, in 1937, at age 55.
- After decades of study, British naturalist Charles Darwin published his revolutionary ideas about nature in 1859, when he was 50.
- U.S. businessman and inventor Steve Jobs, the cofounder of Apple, made the company a worldwide success after returning as its chief executive officer (CEO) in 1997, at age 42.
- Italian artist Leonardo da Vinci painted his most famous work, *Mona Lisa*, in his fifties.

Mid-air emergency

In 2009, 57-year-old airline pilot Chesley Sullenberger made headlines after his plane hit a flock of birds and came down over New York City. Sullenberger's experience and smart decisions helped him crash-land the plane safely in the Hudson River, avoiding numerous skyscrapers and saving all 155 passengers and crew.

Brain and mind studies

The study of the mind is called psychology, from the Greek words psyche (meaning "soul" or "self") and logos (meaning "study"). Austrian scientist Sigmund Freud, who developed many of its central ideas in the early twentieth century, is sometimes called the "father of psychology."

Freud said that children's minds develop in three stages: first comes the id, which controls basic, instinctive needs and desires; then comes the ego, which is a sense of self and others, behavior, and consequences; and at five or six years of age comes the superego, which is the sense of right and wrong. Freud also said that the mind includes conscious thoughts that people are aware of, unconscious processes that are hidden to us, and the subconscious, which people are not fully aware of, but which can influence conscious behavior.

Modern psychologists do not necessarily agree with everything Freud said, but some of his basic ideas match up with what we now know about how brain parts like the amygdala and frontal lobe develop.

Brain scanning

Since the 1970s, scientists have invented several methods for scanning living brains to see how they work. One of the most widely used is called functional magnetic resonance imaging, or fMRI. It uses a magnetic field to make tiny bits called molecules in the brain twist around, then it collects the energy signals they give off, revealing where different substances are in the brain. Increased brain activity uses up extra oxygen. An fMRI can detect this extra oxygen and therefore show where the brain is most active—while a normal MRI scan shows only the brain's structure.

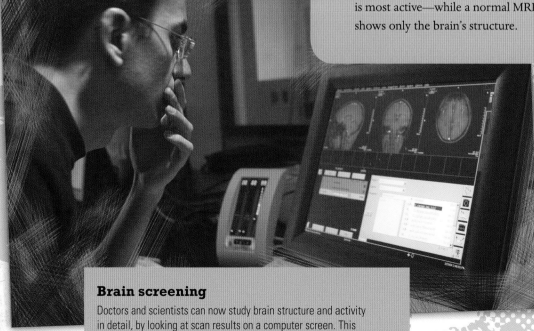

Brain screening

Doctors and scientists can now study brain structure and activity in detail, by looking at scan results on a computer screen. This researcher is viewing scans of a brain taken from different angles.

Science of the mind

The brain and mind are complex and hard to understand—and brain and mind studies have only become major branches of science quite recently. Even more recently, modern technology has allowed us to look inside the brain while it is working.

Mind control

Wouldn't it be great if you could use your mind to control your surroundings—to switch on a light or open a door, for example? Scientists are now developing "mind-reading" technology that can pick up brain signals and link them to buttons on a computer screen. With a special headset on, people can learn to "push" a virtual button just by thinking about it. The buttons can then be linked to real-life devices.

This can be used in computer gaming or to let people who cannot move their bodies control a wheelchair. One day, we could all be using something similar for everyday tasks.

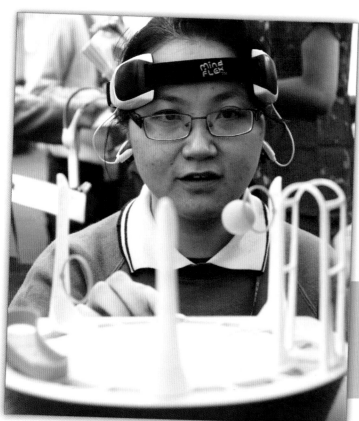

Use your head

This visitor to a science show is trying out a game that is controlled by brain signals.

Brain of a genius

After the great scientist Albert Einstein died in 1955, his brain was preserved. Later, in the 1990s, scientists studied it carefully. They found it was actually slightly smaller than average! But one area, the parietal lobe (see page 8), which deals with mathematical and spatial calculations, was 15 percent bigger. However, scientists do not know if Einstein was born that way, making him a genius, or if the way he thought made that part of his brain develop unusually.

Old Age

No matter how long we live, the mind keeps changing and, in some ways, developing. In some societies, it is assumed that older people lose their mental abilities and lose touch with the world around them. Although this can happen, it is actually not normal. It is possible for people to maintain powerful mental skills and stay mentally active into their seventies, eighties, and nineties.

Gray power

In the modern world, more and more people are continuing to work, create, or play an important part in their society well into old age, a phenomenon sometimes known as gray power:

- British naturalist and TV presenter David Attenborough is famous for making TV shows well into his eighties.
- South African politician Nelson Mandela became president in 1994, at age 75, and he was still active in politics into his nineties.
- In his seventies, U.S. fashion designer Ralph Lauren is still at the forefront of fashion.
- The famous U.S. rock band the Beach Boys was still touring and performing when several band members were in their seventies.

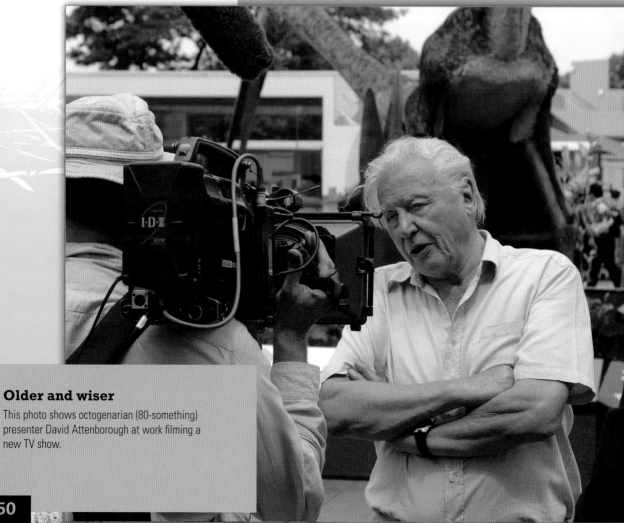

Older and wiser

This photo shows octogenarian (80-something) presenter David Attenborough at work filming a new TV show.

Happiness peaks at age 74

How happy?

For a study, people were asked to rate their own happiness, from 1 (unhappy) to 7 (perfectly content). This graph shows the results.

Older and happier

A recent study asking people how happy they were with their lives concluded that the happiest age of all is 74 (see the graph above). That might seem surprising if you think of old age as a bad thing, but it actually reveals how many older people have very busy, fulfilled lives. The stresses of working and raising a family are usually over, and people have time and freedom to do what they really enjoy. They may also have learned from experience to enjoy what they have, rather than longing for what they do not have, as can happen earlier in life.

Older and wiser

Are older people really wiser? And what is wisdom? Wisdom is a difficult thing to define, but it could be described as a kind of calm, thoughtful common sense, gained through lots of life experience. Crystallized intelligence (see page 46) keeps growing throughout life, and older people tend to have a lot of knowledge and a large vocabulary—but there is more to wisdom than this. Some studies have found, for example, that older people are better than younger people at understanding and solving conflicts and problems between people. They are better at seeing that everyone has opinions and that there may be no "right" answer, and they are also good at coming up with compromises.

Keeping an active mind

There are some things that all people can do as they get older to keep their brains and minds working as well as possible:

- Learn a new hobby, language, or instrument.
- Explore new places.
- Keep track of news, current affairs, art, science, and music.
- Play board games or do crosswords or other puzzles.
- Be creative—for example, paint, sew, or craft.
- Keep physically active.

Slowing down

As people age, their body parts can start to get worn out or weaker—so it is not surprising that this can also happen to the brain. In old age, some of the brain's neurons die or are damaged and can cluster into hardened areas called plaques. Other neurons work less quickly than they used to. The brain also shrinks in old age and can become 10 percent lighter at the age of 90 than it was at age 20.

Missing memory

Short-term memory usually gets worse in older people. For example, your grandpa might tell you the same thing several times, not realizing he has told you it before. However, long-term memories are not wiped out as easily. Memories like a favorite teacher's name or a wedding day were stored when the brain was much younger and more plastic, and so they became more permanent.

Brain problems

For some people, serious brain diseases can strike in old age. One of the best known is Alzheimer's disease. This fatal disease destroys neurons and brain chemicals, causing memory loss, confusion, and mood swings. As it progresses, memories and personality seem to disappear, so that the sufferers are no longer "themselves."

No one is sure what causes Alzheimer's, but scientists have shown that it is less likely in people who are better educated, exercise, eat healthily, and do not smoke and who keep their minds as active as possible.

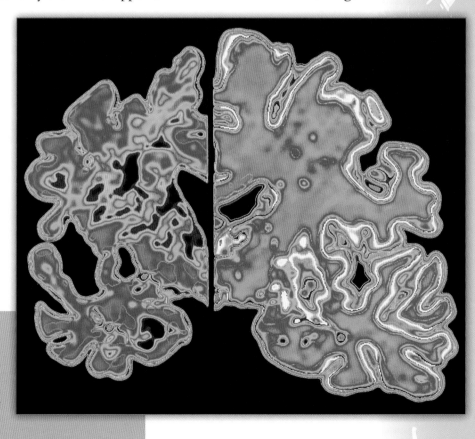

Alzheimer's damage

These scans show a brain damaged by Alzheimer's disease (left), alongside a normal, healthy brain (right).

Strokes

Strokes are also more common in old age. A stroke is like a heart attack in the brain. It happens when a blood clot or burst blood vessel damages or destroys neurons by cutting off their blood supply. Depending on where in the brain this happens, it can cause different effects in a person, such as being unable to speak, recognize people, or move one side of the face or body.

The strange world of strokes

Strokes can affect the brain in some very odd ways. Although this can be awful for the sufferer, it can help scientists to understand more about how the brain works and which parts do what. These are some of the symptoms that stroke patients have suffered:

- They are unable to form new sentences, but they get every word correct when singing old songs.
- They are only able to see the left or right half of their field of view, even though both eyes work.
- They are unable to name familiar objects or figure out how the objects are used.

Stroke recovery

After a stroke, doing specially designed activities and puzzles can help the patient to retrain their brain and make a good recovery.

Mental health

In old age, people are quite likely to suffer the loss of a wife or husband, sibling, or friend. They may also become stuck at home and isolated because of physical health problems. Grieving or feeling isolated are risk factors for depression. Although many people have a very happy old age, depression is more common over the age of 65 than it is at younger ages.

The end of life

As people reach old age, everyone has to deal with something overwhelming: the fact that they will die before long. Of course, it is very hard to know exactly what happens to the brain and mind when we die, and different people have different ideas about it.

What is death?

It is actually quite hard to pinpoint the dividing line between life and death—and the definition of death is different in different countries. People can be considered dead if all parts of the brain have stopped working and they cannot possibly recover, even though they may still be on a life support machine that allows them to breathe. This is often called brain death or brain stem death. The brain stem (see page 9) controls the most basic functions like breathing, so if it has died, there can be no recovery.

In this situation, life support machines are sometimes switched off to allow a person's body to die naturally. But in some cases, people have been kept alive in a state of brain death for many years, while relatives and lawyers try to decide what to do.

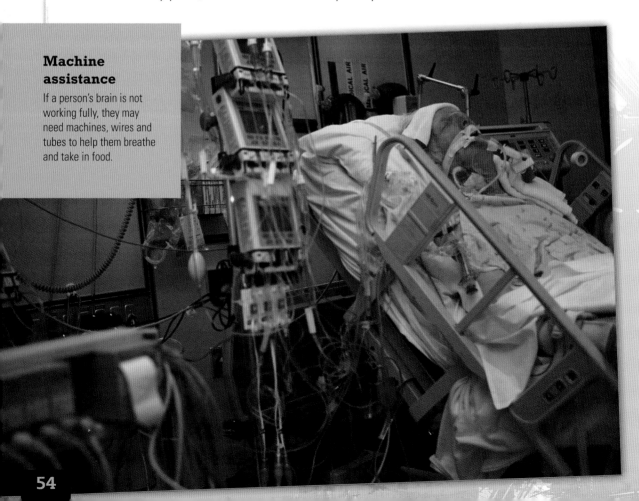

Machine assistance

If a person's brain is not working fully, they may need machines, wires and tubes to help them breathe and take in food.

Death and the mind

What is it like for the mind to experience death? This is one of life's great mysteries. There is no ethical way for doctors and scientists to study it, and scientists do not know what, if any, part of our minds might survive death. But some people who have come very close to death have reported some strange phenomena:

- **"My life flashed before my eyes":** It is common for people who have thought they were about to die—for example, when falling off a cliff—to report that they suddenly recalled everything that had ever happened in their lives. It could be that in extreme fear, the brain goes into overdrive, triggering all of a person's memories at once.

- **A bright light:** People who have almost died sometimes say they felt like they were going down a tunnel toward a bright light. Some scientists think this could be a memory of being born, or it could just be a result of increased electrical activity in the brain.

- **Out-of-body experiences:** Other people have reported that when close to death, they "floated" upward and could see their own body from above. However, scientists think this may be more like a dream, as people having out-of-body experiences do not seem to take in real information from their surroundings, such as what objects are on high shelves in the room.

AMAZING BUT TRUE!

Beheaded brains

In 1905, French scientist Gabriel Beaurieux observed a criminal, Henri Languille, being beheaded by a guillotine (a machine with a heavy blade). He claimed that Languille's face twitched for several seconds afterward and that he reacted when Beaurieux called his name. Beaurieux said: "I called in a strong, sharp voice: 'Languille!' I saw the eyelids slowly lift up ... Next, Languille's eyes very definitely fixed themselves on mine."

But can the mind really stay conscious after beheading? Scientists now think that facial movements after death are probably just the result of nerves receiving random signals as the brain shuts down.

Tests and Puzzles

Quiz

Find out how much you remember about the mental development we experience throughout our lives by completing this quiz. You will find the answers on page 63.

1. Where did Aristotle think thoughts and feelings came from?

2. What is the gap between two neurons called?

3. How many neurons are there in a human brain (approximately)?

   a.) 1 million b.) 100 million
   c.) 100 billion

4. Babies can learn and remember before they are born.
   True or false?

5. Do you need more sleep when you are a.) older or b.) younger?

6. The process of removing some brain connections and strengthening others is called:
   a.) synaptic snipping
   b.) synaptic pruning
   c.) synaptic eliminating

7. What theory does the Sally-Anne test check?

8. Who was blasted through the brain by an iron bar, but survived?

9. What job does the pituitary gland do?
   a.) controls the release of hormones
   b.) sorts out memories
   c.) processes sad emotions

10. Only boys suffer from ADHD.
    True or false?

11. What does alcohol do to reaction times?
    a.) slows them down
    b.) speeds them up

12. Who became known as the "father of psychology"?

13. Albert Einstein's brain was smaller than average.
    True or false?

14. What did scientists discover about the age of 74?

IQ test

These questions are typical of real intelligence quotient (IQ) tests. How well do you score out of 5? You will find the answers on page 63.

1. Which number comes next in the sequence?
   1 - 1 - 2 - 3 - 5 - 8 - ?

2. Which word is missing from the sequence?
   Apple - Banana - _____ - Dog - Elephant

   Choices: Orange   Cabbage   Mouse   Bone   Egg

3. If all monsters are green, and Spike is green, is Spike a monster?

Yes   No   It is impossible to tell

4. If the third day of the month is a Thursday, then the 21st day of the month is a Tuesday.

True or false?

5. Which shape comes next in the sequence?

Brain illusions

These illusions reveal some strange things about the ways our minds work and the mistakes the brain can make.

Lying lines

Which horizontal line is longest, A or B?

They are actually both the same length. The other lines fool your brain into making them look different.

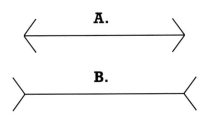

Hermann grid

Look at this image. Are the spaces between the black squares white or not?

This illusion, called the Hermann Grid, makes your brain "fill in" the intersections between the squares with gray dots—but only when you are not looking directly at them.

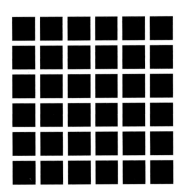

The dabbit

What's this—a duck or a rabbit?

Most people can see both, but not at the same time. The brain wants to settle on one interpretation, so it "flickers" between the two options.

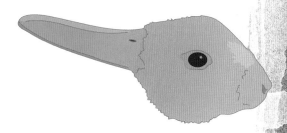

Brain and Mind Timeline

8 months before birth
Brain begins to form.

3 months before birth
Baby in the womb can learn different sounds.

Birth
Brain has 100 billion neurons.

Newborn baby
Brain begins making millions of new connections between neurons.

1–2 months
Babies begin to smile at other people.

3 years
The hippocampus is fully developed, aiding long-term memory storage.

18–24 months
Babies can recognize themselves in a mirror.

12 months
Talking and walking begin around now, on average.

5–8 months
Babies begin to pick up objects.

3–6 months
Babies begin to babble.

5 years
Most children pass the Sally-Anne test and have theory of mind.

10 years
An average child has learned 15,000 words.

10–12 years
A period of intense synaptic pruning begins.

12–13 years
A language learning "window" closes.

13 years
The brain stops growing in size.

25 years
The adult brain is fully developed.

20–25 years
Fluid intelligence peaks.

17–18 years
Criminal behavior peaks in some people.

13–25 years
The brain is especially at risk of damage from drugs and alcohol.

13–18 years
The brain becomes less plastic, permanently storing what is learned.

25–30 years
The average age for the onset of schizophrenia, for those who will suffer from it.

45–55 years
Crystallized intelligence peaks.

65 years
The risk of depression increases.

74 years
Happiness peaks, on average.

78 years
The average lifespan in the United States and Europe.

Brain Science Timeline

4000 BCE
First known written mention of the brain, in ancient Sumerian texts.

2500 BCE
Ancient Egyptians think the heart controls the body and that the brain is unimportant.

2000 BCE
Early peoples use trepanning (drilling holes in the skull) to cure illnesses.

450 BCE
The ancient Greek Alcmaeon is the first to suggest that thoughts are located in the brain.

335 BCE
Aristotle claims thoughts and feelings are located in the heart.

1791
Luigi Galvani discovers that electrical signals pass through nerves and control muscles.

1664
Scientist Thomas Willis identifies many important brain parts.

1649
Philosopher René Descartes states that the brain is a separate thing from the mind.

1543 CE
Andreas Vesalius publishes detailed drawings of the brain, as well as other body parts.

300 BCE
Herophilus studies the brain and decides it is the center of thinking and learning.

1848
Phineas Gage's personality changes after an iron bar damages his frontal lobe.

1862
Paul Broca discovers Broca's area, the part of the brain responsible for forming speech.

1874
Carl Wernicke discovers Wernicke's area, a brain area used for understanding speech.

1880–1900
Early psychological studies begin, and mental illnesses are identified.

1900–1920
Sigmund Freud and others develop ideas about dreams, desires, and parts of the mind.

1930s
Lobotomy (a procedure that involves cutting through the connections between the frontal lobe and the rest of the brain) is developed as a treatment for mental illness. It was meant to calm extreme emotions, but it could have the result of leaving patients emotionless.

1929
The electro-encephalograph (EEG), for reading electrical brain waves, is developed.

1920s
Scientists discover how neurons pass on signals.

1905
Psychologist Alfred Binet introduces early intelligence measurements.

1953
Scientists discover REM sleep.

1972
Invention of magnetic resonance imaging (MRI), to scan brains.

1974
Invention of the positron emission tomography (PET) brain scanning method.

1990
Invention of functional magnetic resonance imaging (fMRI), to scan brain activity.

2010
Researchers develop mind-reading headset technology.

Glossary

adolescence stage of life between childhood and adulthood, from about age 12 to age 19

amygdala part of the brain that processes strong reactions and emotions, such as fear

anorexia nervosa mental illness that makes people want to avoid eating

attention deficit/hyperactivity disorder (**ADHD**) condition that makes it hard to concentrate or stay still

autism condition that makes it hard to understand social rules and fit in with other people

bipolar disorder mental illness that makes the sufferer swing between depression and mania, a state of high energy and excitement

brain stem lower part of the brain that connects the brain to the spinal cord and the rest of the body

cell one of the tiny units that living things are built from

cerebellum area at the back of the brain that deals with balance and movement

conscious aware or awake

consciousness awareness of one's own thoughts and sense of self

corpus callosum bundle of nerves linking the two sides of the brain together

cortex wrinkled outer layer of the brain, used for thinking and information processing

crystallized intelligence type of intelligence based on knowledge and wisdom developed over time

depression mental illness that causes feelings of hopelessness, numbness or worthlessness

dyslexia condition that makes reading and writing difficult

embryo name for a baby in the early stages of development in the womb

endorphin type of brain chemical that can reduce pain and increase feelings of well-being

fluid intelligence type of intelligence involving fast thinking, analysis, and abstract ideas

frontal cortex front part of the cortex, used for personality and rational thought

frontal lobe front section of the brain

gene instructions in cells that are passed on from one generation to the next

gray matter name for the cortex, the part of the brain that deals with thinking and decision-making

hippocampus part of the brain involved in processing emotions and storing memories

hormone chemical released in the body to control the way it works

hypothalamus part of the brain that controls hormones and basic body functions such as temperature

instinct behavior and responses that are built into people's genes, such as blinking in a bright light

irrational not making sense or based on logical reasoning

limbic system cluster of parts found in the middle of the brain, including the amygdala and hippocampus

long-term memory memory that is stored permanently or almost permanently

mental to do with the mind

neurochemical chemical that helps neurons pass on messages in the brain

neuron brain cell that can pass signals to and from other neurons

obsessive compulsive disorder (OCD) illness that makes people obsessed with things like tidiness, symmetry, or repeating rituals

parietal lobe part of the brain involved in math, language, space, and distance

phobia extreme and irrational fear of something

pituitary gland part of the brain involved in releasing hormones

plastic able to be molded or changed

prefrontal cortex part of the cortex at the front of the brain, involved in rational decisions

psychologist scientist or doctor who studies the brain or treats mental illnesses

rational making sense, or based on logical reasoning

REM sleep short for "rapid eye movement" sleep, it is the stage of sleep when the eyes dart around quickly while closed, when most dreaming happens

schizophrenia mental illness that can make people hear voices inside their heads or imagine conspiracies

self-esteem feelings of self-worth and value

serotonin brain chemical involved in feelings of happiness and contentment

short-term memory memory that is kept for a few hours or days, but then forgotten

SSRI short for "selective serotonin re-uptake inhibitor," a type of drug used to treat some mental illnesses

synapse tiny gap between two neurons that signals can jump across

synaptic pruning process of strengthening some connections in the brain, while removing others

theory of mind ability to understand that other people have their own mind and viewpoint

unconscious part of the mind that people are not aware of

Find Out More

Books

Engdahl, Sylvia. *Mental Health* (*Issues on Trial*). Farmington Hills, Mich.:
Greenhaven/Gale Cengage Learning, 2010.

Farrell, Courtney. *Mental Disorders* (*Essential Issues*). Edina, Minn.: ABDO, 2010.

Haddon, Mark. *The Curious Incident of the Dog in the Night-Time*.
New York: Doubleday, 2003.

Mooney, Carla. *Mental Illness Research* (*Inside Science*). San Diego: ReferencePoint, 2012.

Spilsbury, Richard. *The Brain and Nervous System* (*Human Machine*).
Chicago: Heinemann Library, 2008.

Szabo, Ross, and Melanie Hall. *Behind Happy Faces: Taking Charge of Your Mental Health,
a Guide for Young Adults*. Los Angeles: Volt, 2007.

Winston, Robert M. L. *What Goes On in My Head?* New York: Dorling Kindersley, 2010.

Web sites

www.dls.ym.edu.tw/chudler/neurok.html
This large, interactive site is about the brain and nervous system, with facts, pictures, activities,
and experiments.

kidshealth.org/kid/feeling/index.html
This site provides lots of links exploring the mind, feelings, thoughts, and behavior, including
mental illnesses.

kidshealth.org/kid/htbw/brain.html
This is a clear, fun guide to the brain, with illustrations and animations.

www.pbs.org/wnet/brain/index.html
This PBS site accompanies its TV series on brain development, with lots of links and information.

Places to visit

American Museum of Natural History
Central Park West at 79th Street, New York, New York 10024
www.amnh.org, "Brain: The Inside Story" is an amazing exhibition about the brain, including
senses, thoughts, feelings, and mental development.

The Exploratorium
3601 Lyon Street, San Francisco, California 94123
www.exploratorium.edu, The "Mind" exhibition explores thinking and feeling, with dozens
of interactive features.

The Health Museum
1515 Hermann Drive , Houston, Texas 77004
www.mhms.org, This museum offers interactive exhibits about the body and health.

Topics to research

Language

Language is a fascinating phenomenon that is thought to be one of the things that separates humans from other living things. Why does a baby learn to speak just by listening and copying, while a pet cat living in the same house does not? Are there any animals that can talk or learn human languages? Can you find out about any other species that have different sounds for different meanings, similar to the way we use words?

Dreams

Usually, in a dream, we are not aware that we are dreaming—everything seems real. But some people say they can dream "lucidly" and control what happens. Could you do this yourself? And can what you eat before bedtime really affect your dreams? How do your everyday worries, experiences, or relationships crop up in your dreams? You could keep a dream diary, in which you write down the dreams you can remember every morning, to see how they relate to your life.

The puzzle of consciousness

This is a big one! Scientists are still arguing and puzzling over what "consciousness" actually is. What do you think it is? Research some of the theories on how consciousness works and how the brain can be aware of itself. Could machines or networks such as the Internet ever become conscious—and if so, how?

Quiz answers (see pages 56–57)

1) The heart.
2) A synapse.
3) c.
4) True.
5) b.
6) b.
7) Theory of mind.
8) Phineas Gage.
9) a.
10) False. ADHD is more common in boys, but girls can also suffer from it.
11) a.
12) Sigmund Freud.
13) True.
14) It is the age at which people are happiest, on average.

IQ test (see pages 56–57)

1) 13. Each number is the previous two numbers added together.
2) Cabbage. The words are in alphabetical order.
3) It is impossible to tell.
4) False. It is a Monday.
5) Square. The shapes have an increasing number of points, from 0 to 4.

Index

Discarded